JUST BEING AT THE PIANO

JUST BEING
AT THE PIANO

Mildred Portney Chase
FOREWORD BY LEE STRASBERG

PEACE   PRESS

Peace Press, Inc.
3828 Willat Avenue
Culver City, California 90230

9 8 7 6 5 4 3 2 1

Front and back cover photographs by Douglas L. Hamilton.
Typesetting by Freedmen's Organization, Los Angeles.
Printed in the United States of America by Peace Press.

Library of Congress Cataloging in Publication Data

Chase, Mildred Portney.
    Just being at the piano.

    Bibliography
    1. Piano—Instruction and study. I. Title.
MT225.C5   786.3'041   80–8999
ISBN 0–915238–44–6 (bound)   AACR2
ISBN 0–915238–45–4 (pbk.)

T O BE A pianist, in one sense of the word, is to think that a daddy longlegs on the window sill is dancing to your playing; it is to think that the breeze came through the window just to talk to your music; it is to feel that one phrase loves another; it is to think that the tree is a teacher of the tranquility you need in your playing. It is to know a loneliness that is crowded with the beautiful as you play.

D ESIRING TO SHARE some aspects of my own
learning and teaching experience, I dedicate this
book to the students, who have the right to know joy at
each level of growth, and the freedom to individualize
their training for themselves; the interested parents, who
desire to better understand how to be helpful to the effort;
and to the teachers, who complete this eternal triangle,
and can cast light on learning in a way to allow its beam to
extend the length of life itself.

ACKNOWLEDGMENTS

THIS BOOK IS what it is because of the teachers of my own learning: Victor Trerice, Olga Steeb, Josef Lhevinne, Rosina Lhevinne, Richard Buhlig, Josef Rosenfeld; the students whom I have taught, and the influence of Eastern thought on all I thought I knew.

I might not have written this book had I not been encouraged to do so and helped in many ways when I needed it by my husband Bill and our two sons, Kenneth and Sanders, and also by Bob Beebe, Leonora Panich, Betty Goldwater, Rena Gordon, Marcia Waldorf, Peter Yates, and Lynne Wilson.

My deepest appreciation to my editor, Deborah Lott. Her mastery of the craft was combined with an ability to tune into the thoughts of the writer. Her sympathetic ways were of immeasurable help in the task. Thanks also to all those at Peace Press for their confidence and support.

My special thanks to Allen Chabin of *Westwood Book Store* and Stan Madson and Marc Labinger of *the Bodhi Tree* for taking a chance on an earlier version of this book.

Even though they did not live to see this book, my mother and father, Sarah and Marcus Portney, and my friend of a lifetime, Genevieve DeVore, have a place in these pages and in my heart.

My love and appreciation to all.

CONTENTS

FOREWORD

I AM NOT a musicologist nor do I have any technical knowledge of music. I do not play an instrument, a lack I have often deplored. But I love music, instrumental or vocal, especially the solo voice or the solo instrument, especially the piano. Since I am unable to approach music directly through my own efforts, I enjoy and appreciate only through the performances of those technically trained to convey their sense of what the music is all about. I have amassed a large collection of music on records from the early days of recording to the present. I have no way of judging the purely technical skill and it is instead the music and the spirit conveyed in it to which I respond.

The spiritual quality of a performance is something beyond the external technique which is today so highly prized and which develops highly skillful performers often without any clear, personal attitude to their work. I can appreciate technique only in terms of percussive quality or speed and so on, but the piano is essentially a percussive instrument and yet you want to make it *sing*, and that is very, very difficult and goes beyond technique.

In all art, the thing that differentiates the skillful tech-nician from the artist is the presence of an experience that vitalizes, that *brings alive* what would be otherwise only a surface rendering. Music is written to express something and the pianist who plays it must not just play the notes but must be able somehow to express what the notes are related to. In general today, there is too much emphasis on external skills. In the past, great pianists didn't mind mak-ing false notes. In fact, Schnabel once permitted a record to be published and simply explained that there were false notes in it. "Why don't you correct it?" he was asked. He said, "I want the public to see that I am human. Besides, that performance was better than another that didn't have those wrong notes."

It seems to be true that part of the dissatisfaction on the part of young people today arises from the fact that most of what they are taught is simply a process of mental memory, of repeating what they have been told and that they are not encouraged to experience what they should have con-tact with, so that they can express their own attitude in relation to what they have been taught.

I respond emphatically to Mildred Portney Chase's at-tempts to get away from the purely technical approach to playing the piano and to stress the spiritual elements of the performance. While I have no musical expertise, I am a teacher and trainer of talent with some degree of experi-ence and accomplishment in dealing with the most intrac-table material of all: the actor who has no instrument outside of himself with which to deal.

In our work with actors, we refer to those elements that are not simply the external parts of the craft but which derive from sensitivity, experience, thought, the use of conscious or unconscious experience that frees you at the moment of creation. We speak in terms of mental experience, which is the thought processes that lead to activity, and in terms of sensory experience, which is some awareness of a reality which we ourselves may often be insufficiently cognizant of, but which always accompanies whatever we're doing. And we speak in terms of emotional experience, which for me, is the groundwork of all art.

When I first read an early draft of *Just Being at the Piano*, I was intrigued by certain similarities between Chase's approach and my own. She is also committed to freeing the performer's energies at the moment of creation. She stresses the importance of the sensory experience and the emotional experience, attempting to sensitize the pianist to the experience of playing as it happens. Her emphasis on the psychological problems of the student, and for that matter, the performer, seem eminently suitable. She recognizes the need for relaxation, for a step-by-step approach, for a solution to the student's individual problems, for permitting each student to progress at his or her own pace. She works towards developing the musician's sensory awareness of the sound, of the touch, of what the entire body is experiencing, so that each tone may sing.

These and many other suggestions in *Just Being at the Piano* are confirmed by the modern psychological rather than the purely mechanical approach to the problem of learning to play the piano.

LEE STRASBERG

INTRODUCTION

I AM CONTINUALLY finding my way toward the *here and now* in my music and realizing a whole new dimension to the experience of playing. Nowhere is it more important to be in the here and now than in playing the piano. The slightest lapse in attention will affect every aspect of how I realize the recreation of a piece of music. One note, coming a hair's breadth late in time, may distort the expression of a phrase. It is impossible to be self-conscious and totally involved in the music at the same time. Consciousness of the self is a barrier between the player and the instrument. As I forget my own presence, I attain a state of oneness with the activity and become absorbed in a way that defies the passage of time.

Each time we play, we are new beings, and the performance that was fitting yesterday does not have the ring of truth today—even if we were to be able to identically duplicate it. Spontaneity in playing is all important; only a recording will play over and over again and sound exactly the same.

This book is about being able to experience the instant at the time of its being. Much of it was written at the piano during practice. As I discovered a new awareness or as an insight came to me I would make a brief notation. Before I began to keep a journal at the piano, awakenings would come over me, be forgotten, and then return again some-times years later. I finally brought a writing pad to the piano and whenever an idea took hold, I made a note. This helped me to remember the experience of a particular moment and to share it with others.

In my own experience I dared to let go and I dared to forget, and even though I was fearful, I was driven to move this way. I had to let go of a way of playing that was secure, based upon years of study. In letting go of a way of playing which had held up well enough even in concerts, I often wondered if I was losing my way, never to find it again and never to reach another that I could accept in its place. Sometimes I even wondered if this journey was rational. It was easy to become discouraged. I discovered ways that would work for a while and then later fail to serve me well. But there was a tenacity that never left me, along with a healthy degree of anxiety. All this was necessary in order to allow the insights which eventually proved to be the missing parts in what I had been taught. These were the parts that only I could fill in, that could only be learned from myself. What I discovered as I went on served to give me that sense of involvement on a deep level that I had known to be missing. I am indebted to writings on Zen and Taoism. From these I drew threads of awareness in new directions and found much that was compatible with what I was discovering at the piano.

Artists in any field of expression can undergo great lone-liness and feel separated from the more ordinary endeavors in life. They can resent the fact that their efforts do not seem needed or wanted by our society. A plumber, a foot-ball coach, a beautician, let alone the lawyer or doctor—all have a more legitimate place in this world. I have felt my share of resentment for being in this position. Through the process of growth taking place I finally am better able to realize the true reward of my art: living in a constant state of discovery and increased awareness.

I am now able to reach a state of being at the piano from which I come away renewed and at peace with myself, having established a harmony of the mind, heart, and body. This does not diminish my performance in any way, either in style or in communicativeness. In fact, it is quite the opposite. The heightened awareness and the sense of harmony that I take away with me from the instrument benefit the people with whom I interact, and the other activities that occupy me. We bring to our music from our lives and take from our music to the rest of our living.

I no longer feel tormented as I used to when I am unable to fit in my hours of practice. Now even if I have only fifteen minutes at the piano on an extremely busy day, if I can reach this state of harmony in my playing even briefly, I leave the instrument knowing that I have experienced the heightened moment, and to touch on it will nourish the rest of the day.

Just being—at the piano—egoless—is to each time seek to reach that place where the only thing that exists is the sound and moving toward the sound. The music on the page that was outside of you is now within you, and moves through you; you are a channel for the music, and play from the center of your being. Everything that you have consciously learned, all of your knowledge, and the feelings evoked by that knowledge, emanate from within you. There is a sense of oneness in which the heart of the musician and the heart of the composer meet, in which there is no room for self-conscious thought. You are at one with yourself and the act, and feel as if the playing has already happened and you are effortlessly releasing it. The music is in your hands, in the air, in the room, the music is everywhere, and the whole universe is contained in the experience of playing.

ATTITUDE

ALMOST ALL OF us can number among our
childhood friends one or more who studied the piano.
Out of their homes would come the sounds of their practice, filtering through the voices of friends playing outdoors. In the home, the family would come to enjoy an
often repeated piece, and at school, classmates and teachers
would enjoy the "finished" results of practice. All too
often, along the way, these sounds ceased. If there were a
way to recapture these sounds and all the sounds of piano
practice that ever traveled through the air, touched off by
countless aspirants lured by the desire to play music, and if
there were a way to link these sounds together, they surely
would trace a sound path from the earth to the moon.

Time spent at the piano can be an insightful journey
inward, the pleasure deepening with the years. The joy of
the moment can be experienced at any stage of learning.
We need only to recognize when we are guided away from
ourselves by standards of performance based on comparison with others, or by the need of approval and recognition for accomplishment. Too often these motivations

dominate the learning environment. Far too many fine instruments remain untouched and soundless. If these instruments were to play again, might not an objective listener prefer the sounds issuing from more modest efforts to the insistent and relentless type of practice that can be heard frequently in any serious conservatory? The professional may even envy the practicing and free improvising of one who plays solely out of love and for her own pleasure. The so-called amateur may play from the heart even if her proficiency is not on the highest level.

In a world that saturates our minds with its ills, more than ever we need to explore the aesthetic aspects of life in order to better focus our own lives, and to gain some sense of equilibrium. Many of us are moving toward a philosophical approach, based on Eastern thought which emphasizes harmony and unity. These concepts are not only highly compatible, but necessary, if we are to realize what involvement in the arts has to offer us. A process of self-realization can take place if we study in a way that allows for the natural unfolding of the individual.

Even within the highly disciplined demands of the study of music, the tight net of knowledge and expectation can be loosened. That which we have consciously learned can be intuitively released in our playing: *Thinking* becomes *Feeling.* As learning takes hold, the directorial mind "backs off." No longer right on top of the action, the mind allows space for feeling and intuition to enter. The self observes with a glancing look rather than with a rigidly focused eye. You may come to a learning situation with expectations but without self-acceptance. It is as though someone drew a circle around your life and you were expected to reach its circumference which, paradoxically, circumvents your reaching.

Starting with the *here and now* and taking just this instant, letting ourselves into it and being with it only, can free us of expectation. If we do not expect to have knowledge at the outset, we are open to the desire *to know* and to explore and discover and grow. If we can simply accept where we are for the moment, then we are freed from self-condemnation.

Love is the most important quality to bring to any task. Love draws all that we have within us to the action in which we are involved. It brings trust and acceptance; it heightens the senses; it allows us to be completely immersed in our work. Love does not bring forth censorship and defensiveness, conditions that adversely affect our learning ability. It allows self-acceptance and total involvement.

Any negative state of mind affects the quality of our work. Many times, having expected to be at the piano by a certain time, I felt annoyed that I still had not completed my chores. I unknowingly carried this state of mind with me to the instrument, and did not know why, on these occasions, I did not like my playing. I realized that I brought whatever state of mind I was in with me to the piano. I couldn't bring anger and resentment to the piano and expect to be instantly transformed. Now, when I find myself in this resentful state, being pulled from my work by my desire to practice, I think about how I will feel playing. My whole inner relationship to the task at hand changes.

If I am in the middle of washing dishes, I turn my attention to washing dishes and start *to be with* what I am doing. As my hand moves over each dish, I focus on its surface and follow its form.

Turning it into the water to be rinsed, I notice how I shift its weight in my hand; how I use my hand and arm to perform the various movements. Moving slightly more slowly than usual, I become aware of all the sensations felt in washing dishes; I move in a way that establishes a harmony between myself and the act. Moving in this direction I come to the piano as if already mentally in practice, and I bring something of my music to my everyday tasks, lifting them out of the ordinary and attaining a sense of release from which to begin a meaningful session at the piano.

Anticipating practice can be part of the pleasure of practice. The transition between completing a task and beginning practice can be imbued with music. Even as you adjust the bench and set the music on the rack, you let yourself out of the ordinary and into the mood for making music. Only then can you begin to release those thoughts that block your total involvement. Only from that state of total involvement, can you begin to play in the way in which you dream.

BODY AWARENESS
AND MOVEMENT

E VERY MUSICIAN DREAMS of owning an
instrument that is capable of producing the most beautiful sounds possible. He pursues every lead that he can to
locate this ideal instrument of his imagination. Once he
has chosen the instrument, he begins to explore its potential. The more sensitivity he brings to the instrument, the
more he is able to appeal to possibilities beyond what it
seems to possess.

With the piano, body movement always plays a part.
You need to move in order to create the sound. A feeling
of oneness with the instrument is an ultimate requirement. This will express itself in beautiful movement, that
is, coordination, and will represent a state of harmony
within the person. Any tension that disturbs this state of
harmony will hinder the natural movement.

Recently, a young man began lessons with me. He had a
good understanding of music; years of attending concerts
had influenced his musical taste. Yet, he could not reveal
his feeling for music in his playing. Whenever he placed his
hands on the keys they instantly acquired rigidity. The

coordination between the mind and body was blocked. Fear of not playing well enough got in the way of his love for the music and the instrument. Whatever the reason for its presence, tension interferes with the freedom of movement. This affects the individual tone as well as the flow of a phrase.

Tension has a devious way of taking hold even within a child. A five-year-old hearing a wrong note can giggle, because she is still open enough to hear the "funny" sound. By the time a child is six, the response has already changed. The older child grimaces, shakes her head, or says, "I want to start all over again." The child feels the need to look good and wants approval. She has begun to personalize little failures, the tension becoming more deeply ingrained each time they occur. Children are quickly acculturated to measuring their worth by their performance. Too many adults remain this kind of child all their lives. Sooner or later, they may give up to futility. Interest closes off and apathy becomes one of the layers upon which lack of self-esteem is built. Too many adults can hardly move with grace in their ordinary daily tasks, let alone one as complicated as playing a musical instrument. They cannot rid themselves of tension and be relaxed in their movements. It is not always enough to say, "Relax your wrist; keep it loose. Let your shoulders be free," and so on. Exercises for the purpose of relaxing the body, such as shaking the wrists and shoulders or swinging the arms, may loosen the muscles, but they lack direct connection with the playing of the instrument, or with tuning the mind with the heart and the body.

In a typical example, a student was undergoing a crisis in her life. At her lesson her posture was slumped, expressing her sense of defeat and depression. She lacked emotional energy, so important in producing a good sound. She had brought fairly difficult music with her, and was tense, ill at ease, and hesitant in playing her first piece. She felt intimidated and afraid that I might find fault with her playing. Recognizing the problem, I delayed her playing. I suggested that when she felt the urge to move her hands from her lap to the keys that she do so, but to be very aware of her hands, as though they had a will of their own, and to let them move very slowly to where they wanted to go. If they did not wish to reach the keys, but wanted to move back into her lap, that is where they should be allowed to return. This movement was to be slow, continuous, and flowing; without stops at any point. She carried this out, and upon returning her hands to her lap, she gave out a deep, sighing breath. This sigh expressed a release of tension from deep within. She was learning how to recognize how much emotionally based energy was available to the beginning movement, how much restricted by her tension. To continue the movement beyond the energy that was available would be to unnaturally impose the rest of the movement. The release of emotion helped her to increase the span and go further with the next movement. This exercise is like stretching the body. You can only stretch so far comfortably on the first try. But as you relax, you are able to stretch a little further.

To move when we do not feel the energy to do so is like a singer trying to sing a phrase with insufficient breath. The music should already be within us before the first sound is made and the first move to the keys has to carry in it the "breath" for its sound. The beginning sound is the most important—from it the rest of the phrase emerges; the first phrase affects the next. Trepidation can attend the first phrase even with the most experienced player. He looks to the beginning to give his playing "heart." He wants to be able to move on its inspiration; not to need to warm up as the performance continues, although when necessary, the buoyant spirit can attend this process as well. Recognition of the music, its mood, its tempo, its tonal quality needs to already be awakened and embodied in the first movement to the keys.

In the freeing movement of my student's hands, the emotional debris began to be cleared from the path of motion. She relaxed, and when she moved her hands to the keys again, it was with greater freedom, and the tone was good. Expectation about the sound had hindered her movement, had literally made her rigid. Now the movement seemed to originate from a deeper place within her. (Pablo Casals claimed that when you think you are relaxed, you can still find a part of the body that can be relaxed more.) My student became encouraged with the success of her first experience in releasing tension at the piano. She continued with a freeing movement I describe in this way:

Stand away from the piano, let your arms hang freely. Allow the barest natural swinging to set in. As slight as it may be, let it make you aware of the current of air on which you move. You can learn much from nature. Take a moment to look at a tree. Find the branch that is moving the most quietly. Feel how it might feel, as though a gentle breeze is moving your hands. Your hands may sway gently, back and forth, similar to the way the branch moves. Let this feeling move into your arms, enabling them to increase their span of movement and change directions. Imagine that the breeze is carrying your hands on gently curving paths of air currents. You are releasing your expression through your own individualized calligraphy of movement.

During the course of study, my student learned to recognize when she needed these freeing movements. Inner quiet and integration began to take the place of tension. She sensed a different involvement in her playing. Her playing began to reveal her ability in a way she had not known before.

Another way to tune into a source of effortless energy can be practiced while seated. Place your hands together, touching fingers and palms. Gradually draw them apart in a parallel position, very slowly, until they are extended outwards. Without stopping the movement, bring them towards each other and apart again and continue changing direction at their own sensing. The general movement is akin to an accordion opening and closing.

At some point in returning your hands together you will sense a resistance as though there were a field of negative polarity preventing them from touching. Feel as though your hands are pulling a mass of air with their whole surface. You can feel a change in the temperature of the air and your hands may tingle. You can feel that you are displacing air as you move the hands apart and that they are pressing an air cushion as they come together.

To sensitize your hand and finger movements, open and close one hand, very slowly. Do not stop at any point in the motion. You may want to remove any jewelry heavy enough to impede smooth continuity at the change of direction in the movement. Feel the air to be a substance. As your fingers move away, think that you are pulling air. Experience the sensations fully as your fingers close towards each other without touching. Continue to open and close one hand and then move on to the other, allowing your sense of the air's resistance to awaken.

The following is an exercise that I developed in a practice session of my own. Seated at the piano, touch the keys lightly. Don't think of the sound yet, just the feeling. Imagine an acquarium with plants anchored to the rocks in the water, their tendrils floating. A fish swimming by moves the tendrils, but the roots remain secure. While resting your fingers on the keys, simulate that floating movement in your arms, sensing the qualities of the plant you are visualizing in your mind, feeling your fingers to be as secure as the roots of the plant, your arms to be like the tendrils. Feel your fingers cling to the keys while allowing your hands and arms to move as gently and slowly as the plants in the water. Feel the buoyancy of your arms being supported by the water. Feel utterly free in your movement. Now release and play a note, thinking that you do not have to play the next note in time. Allow a very natural movement to bring your hand to the key, and allow yourself to enjoy the feeling. Imagine that you are able to feel the vibrations in the strings through the keys. Imagine that you can listen through the skin of your fingers, that you are able to feel the vibrations of the strings. Josef Lhevinne suggested imagining that you are actually playing on the wires. In one instance he used the expression "the wires are rung as a bell."

Now gently move your body in the way it feels it wants to, your fingers still resting lightly on the keys. Release your hand movements into the air. Feel the air around you. Feel the space you occupy within it. Open your hands as you are moving and close them slowly and gently. Feel the air as a cushion that is compressed as your fingers move toward each other. Sense a tingling in the hands as the fingers draw away from each other. It is as though the air wants to connect them and you can actually feel them pulling.

This chapter can be a point of departure; you can carry it further, following your own inclination. These self-expressing movements will enable you to approach any task with an increased sense of giving yourself to it. Although these concepts have been developed in connection with playing the piano, you can apply them to playing stringed instruments with special regard to bowing and shifting, and to dance movement in gaining lightness, balance, and grace. Whether moving across the room, sitting down, standing up, or handling an object, there can now be an awareness added to the action which enhances the *here and now*. Nothing you do need any longer feel menial as long as you have this increased awareness.

WARMING UP

E ACH DAY, JUST as we must find ourselves anew in relating to the world, so must we find ourselves anew in relating to the instrument. A dancer does not begin with strenuous movements the first thing in the morning. She begins with a whole session of warming up at the bar, where slowly and sensitively, the body awakens. To bypass the warm up is unthinkable to the dancer. In its own way, the same necessity exists for the pianist, as well as for any other instrumentalist.

There are days when the first playing I do is so far from my liking that I could easily despair. Usually, the worst times are when I am out of practice. Sometimes the pressures of daily obligations are at fault. Yet, usually, I can still find my way again within a relatively short time if I become very aware of the movements I am making.

I find it most helpful to focus on the release. I may play a short phrase and in the release, allow my hands and arms to move away from the instrument and then back again, as a dancer would, with a feeling of grace and fully in contact with the last sound played. Or, I may simply move, using the gesture in choreographed movement to a musical phrase. This may undo any tension that might bind the fingers in playing out the phrase.

Play a short phrase, and let the release continue into the air. Let your hands rise from the keys very slowly. Your hands may turn over and expand outwards. Allow the natural momentum and thrust of the movement to express itself, in a complete release. Move your hands and arms slowly and fluidly, sensing the current of air which supports them. Focus on how your arm feels as it moves through the air, the flow of air between the fingers. Become aware of the sensations of moving through the air, using this space to sensitize your movements; embracing this space in relating to the piano.

Envision your arms as the branches of a tree responding to a mild breeze; your torso bending with the movement yet supportive as the trunk of the tree. Your hands may change course but always with fluidity, tracing graceful, curving movements. This slow, balletic motion allows for the full release of the impulse that was expressed in the playing. Just as a tennis player continues his swing after contacting the ball, you continue the release motion. The movement ends when you feel that the impulse has run out. Then let your hand come to rest in your lap to return to the keys again only when you feel ready. Then repeat the phrase or continue on to the next.

This complete follow-through will make you conscious of the importance of fully releasing one impulse of movement before going into another. To move into a new motion before completely releasing the first is like trying to shift gears without releasing the clutch. In playing, there can be a cumulative jamming of the impulses of movement which can adversely affect the balance and flow of gestures. The impulse for each gesture at the piano is as breath is to the singer. In singing, a phrase may be sung on one breath, and once that breath is spent, the singer will renew it. At the piano, I have the same sense of expressing a single impulse in a movement, releasing it completely, and then renewing the impulse. As the taking of breath originates in the torso and is felt in association with the emotional interpretation of the song, the impulse for movement can be felt to come from the torso, from the heart, and is connected to the emotional interpretation of the music. While the follow-through described here requires large movements in space, its purpose is to sensitize you to eventually have the same feeling of complete release without even lifting your fingers from the keys.

Play the first note of a short difficult group and then repeat it in its own timing. Seek a sense of buoyancy in the release and let it be the feeling with which your hand comes up. See if you can spread this same feeling of buoyancy through your fingers as you play out the rest of the group of notes. In this way you will play all the notes on one impulse without unnecessarily introducing another. There is a danger that the drive or energy from an impulse can leak out of the hand through an unwanted movement. The wrist wants to be centered and fluid so that equalized flexibility will be available for all the movements required of it. The desired economy of movement and expressiveness of the phrase occur naturally. They should not be sought, since the effort of seeking may curb the movement and deprive the phrase of its full expressive contour.

Every skill acquired at the piano can easily involve kinesthetic pleasure. Even though the total act of playing is complex, especially on an advanced level, it consists of many simple natural movements which are dovetailed.

I emphasize release and responsiveness because these elements give us the freedom to pause in our playing without stopping, to provide accent in our playing that is strong but also tender, to express subtle fluctuations of mood. Release and responsiveness bring magic to our playing that exceeds what is indicated on the page.

Whether you start your day's practice with studies or with repertoire, you should sooner gain satisfaction in the session. Even scale practice may be benefitted and become more aesthetically directed.

TONE

LISTENING ... FEELING ... moving ... feeling ... listening. This is how to explore the way to the beautiful, resonant, singing tone. Once you have heard your most beautiful tone and have become aware of the sensations accompanying that sound, your understanding can be adapted to any shortening or lengthening, increasing or decreasing in volume. The core of any tone should always have substance and expressive quality. The singing quality of tone can be developed by sensitizing the ear to listen for it and sensitizing the hands and fingers to feel it as if they too were listening. The communicative presence of the singing tone is always desirable.

In singing, since the individual is the whole instrument, much attention is of necessity given to the sensations involved in producing the sound. Too often, with the pianist, this subject is dwelt on very little or not at all.

The piano is one of the instruments most physically separated from the player; most musical instruments being small enough to be held close to the body. To help overcome this separateness, we need to awaken every response necessary that can be helpful in creating a unity between us and the instrument setting inches away from our bodies.

A child may draw a beautiful line simply out of the enjoyment of doing so, unencumbered by concern for the results. Similarly, a child who has not yet studied, may simply drop his hands on the keys and bring forth a beautiful tone. Perhaps when we were small children, prior to studying, but drawn to the instrument with enchantment, we, too, were able to find these beautiful tones. In the process of learning the placement and the timing and the numerous other things we had to incorporate into our playing, we had to think of too many details and lost that feeling of enchantment. In working towards so-called perfection and absolute accuracy, tonal quality may have taken second place in our consideration. Yet it would seem that to reach for tonal quality would automatically include accuracy and proficiency.

The complex adjustments that take place in any movement in playing can easily be jammed out of fluidity by conscious effort. The spontaneity and freedom of movement may be restricted by the effort, affecting the tonal quality. Can you imagine the gong of a bell creating a beautiful sound if there were any hesitancy in its free swinging? With a singer, hesitancy would immediately be recognized. With the pianist, the sound might not be as unpleasantly affected, but the potential quality would have been robbed.

Knowledge should be laid gently on our work. Only then can we move in the direction of the *effortless effort*, where we can let go of the tight reins of intellect and experience the *here and now*, finding our own way. With knowledge lodged gently in our awareness, we accept the less than perfect without letting that affect our love for our work. We can accept our efforts as honest expressions, which reveal what needs to be changed and gently guide us towards the better sound.

Do not be afraid to reduce your musical experience to one beautiful sound, knowing that it will find its own way through all your playing. Do not be too greedy and grasp at the beautiful sound. Allow it to flow into your consciousness effortlessly. Striving will only force it. Let the awakening of more sensitivity in you decide the course of the tone.

The sculpture is already in the stone and you need only to remove the excess rock to reveal it. In playing all that you have learned intellectually, physically, emotionally is now there with you, and by removing concerns with the outcome of the playing, removing any interfering tension, you will be able to release the music that is within you.

Play a series of tones and let pass all those that are not to your best liking. Observe those you like the most and notice the way you felt and moved when you produced them. Notice every sensation in your body. You are learning from yourself because you are the only one who knows how you obtained this sound. The best teachers in the world, if gathered around your instrument, could not tell you how to find your way to it again. When you think you have gotten the best sound the instrument can bring forth, think a little magic into it, and you may discover a still better sound. The way we think has so much to do with the outcome. Sometimes I may tell a young student to think of a fairy with a magic wand, for even this imagery may suddenly help to transform the student's tone.

You may be visited by a "happy accident" in your playing. A phrase sounds better than you should have expected. When you find yourself suddenly functioning at an enhanced capability for even one phrase, you can learn something that can widen into all of your playing, moving you to a higher level. If you can produce just one beautiful tone, then you can look forward to carrying this quality over two tones, and, in time, being able to maintain it for any length of phrase.

Sometimes I think of the game in which an object is hidden and one person searches for it, while receiving clues from the other players. When he gets closer to the hidden object, his friends tell him, "you are getting warmer," and he then proceeds in that direction. If they indicate the opposite, he shifts direction, trying to sense his proximity to the object. He changes his direction only gradually since he is not sure how far away he is, and would not want to lose his bearings altogether, and have to start from scratch. It is the same with our work at the piano as we seek out and become aware of the better of our sounds. That is the "getting warmer" for us. Since our efforts cannot always be charted ahead of time, we may only sense our way along to a better place. Instead of depending on others to tell us how we are doing, we must listen to our own inner guiding. As in the game, when we are not finding the sounds that are to our liking, it is better for us not to radically reject a course as we change our way. We might deny ourselves the only logical starting place for improvement. If we can accept the tone, knowing that we can eventually move through it to a better tone, we will not lose the feeling from the heart.

We must also consider the requirements of the instrument which plays its part in the creation of the beautiful tone, although not always in the most welcome way. Even with your own piano, the weather may cause the sound to differ from one day to the next. Humidity plays a very large part in this. Each time you go to the instrument, you need to be sensitive to this possibility. Since the instrument cannot do the adjusting, you must. Along with the knowledge that we possess, we need to be accepting enough so that instead of dictating we give way to the senses involved—listening, feeling, moving, and listening. Performing on a strange piano, I have realized the greatest benefits from working in this way. I can remember the anxieties I used to experience every time I performed on a piano that did not please me. I was, each time, bitterly disappointed that months spent in hard practice were sabotaged by an inferior or neglected instrument. It took a long time for me to free myself of this hindering reaction. I am reminded of the story of "Beauty and the Beast." We need to learn to love the beast (which in this instance is the piano). I have learned that when I do not like my tone, but accept it as it is, not fighting it, then I am able to gradually adjust everything toward improving it.

Things that we learn that are beneficial to our playing may slip out of our minds from time to time. Do not let it concern you too much if you forget some of what you have learned. It is surprising how knowledge will float back into consciousness at moments of need, and real desire to know.

Many times I experienced moments of great clarity; a new insight into my playing would come to me and open my understanding. Afterwards trying to recall these awarenesses was like trying to recall a dream; something had been lost in memory. They were so visceral, so tied up to being at the piano that I could not recount them once away from the music. But often the same insight would recur, unexpectedly, when I was playing again.

If you feel resistance to a new idea there is probably a reason for it and it would be against your nature to force it. Let what you learn find its own natural way into your playing. An idea that you are resistant against now may find you later in a more receptive mood or you may suddenly have a new conception of it. Let it find its home in you but do not force it in any way.

Even a few minutes a day devoted to tone consciousness can be beneficial. Do not attempt it for an instant longer than the spirit is willing. Once you find your way to a more beautiful tone you will be drawn to it and will find yourself creating it more and more throughout your practice as your ear becomes more involved.

The various artists of the keyboard disagree on the positions and actions of the whole body as well as the shoulders, arms, elbows, wrists, hands, and fingers. These contradictions are amusing, especially when two superb artists practically cancel out each other's approach, so strongly do they disagree. One may say to hold the elbows close to the body; another will allow movements away from the body. Some describe the movement in playing as a fall, or a pulling fall. Rosina Lhevinne used the expression "come to me" in connection with drawing the sound out of the instrument and dramatized it in a beguiling gesture of the hand.

Schnabel liked to move forward into the keys, but was in favor of letting the hand move in any and all directions, and using flat as well as rounded fingers, depending on the music. Some artists use arched positions of the hand; others, a flat hand. Some use a higher level for the wrist, and others, lower.

They all agree on the importance of relaxation which is of the utmost necessity for good tone as well as facility. Because the physical and mental requirements of playing are so demanding, it is not always easy to be relaxed. That is why even the most accomplished artists may not be entirely free of this concern. Awareness of the space in which we move contributes to relaxation. The space, which is air, is in us as we breathe and around us as we move. If we become conscious of displacing air as we move, and sense that it has resistance and can support our weight, then as the hand falls to the keys, it can move very slowly and without hesitance.

Feel the space as an air cushion supporting the weight of the hand as it moves. This can help you to develop the sense of trust necessary for creating the most delicate tonal quality. The modern piano has more power than we need for most of our playing. To appeal to less than its full power the tendency is to hold back at the same time you're playing. It is important to find a way to play within the softer ranges of tone without holding back. Awareness of the air supporting you slows down your fall into the keys. This is of greatest help in getting the sense of balance and repose so necessary for playing the slow, single tone phrases. These can be harder for the serious artist than the fastest passages with the most notes. The balance necessary in this case is such a delicate requirement; nothing can be hidden with a roll of the hand or pedaling.

Depress the damper pedal. Play a tone, keeping the pedal down. Slowly release the hand from the keys and allow it to float upward, still holding the pedal down. Listen to the sound as it fades and let your hand tune in to this sound. Repeat. Your hand should slowly float up on the same path as the one upon which it went down. Never let the movement stop, and while always in motion, return to play the same key again. Imagine that the tone rises like warm air and follow its path upward with your hand. Your hand rides on the sound. Feel your hand moving in contact with it. Think of the vibrations of the tone as rising—they and your hand are one. As your hand returns to the keys again, imagine that the fingers cling for a fleeting instant as they contact the keys. As your hand moves off the keys, it should feel as though it is gently and smoothly retracing an already established path. The upward movement is a continuation of the downward movement; a slow rebound of the downward movement. It is a follow-through that flows into a new start again, so that sense of continuity is maintained. To produce a living, warm tone, you cannot be cut off anywhere; you want the utmost feeling of fluidity and unity.

Play a low, bass note with the damper pedal down. Keeping the pedal down, repeating the note with one hand for a continuous sound, try the following with the other hand: Lightly touch the strings of the key you have played and feel how strongly it vibrates. On the same sound, touch the strings higher up the scale, moving gradually up higher yet, and see how far up you can still detect the sympathetic vibrations of other strings to the tone you have sounded. If you touch the strings too heavily you will miss out on some of the response you are trying to awaken, so keep a light touch.

Now simply play a low key again, with the pedal down and feel the vibration through the key bed under your finger. Make whatever adjustments in the condition of the finger and hand as are necessary to feel this vibration. You will feel it less and less as you ascend the keyboard but a residue of the feeling will remain and teach you something about the delicate balance of weight on the fingers. Seeking to experience the feeling of the vibrations under your finger will automatically avoid its coming down too hard and will encourage a feeling of release even while holding the key down. Even as you continue to hold the key down you begin to feel the rebound sensation in the hand and arm. Take care not to withhold or interfere with the flow of motion, however slight.

Thinking that you must go to the "bottom of the key" can be detrimental if it restricts the flow and rebound of the movement. Think of working *around* the tone rather than directly *at* it. Consciousness of the follow-through prevents hardness of tone which can result from thinking of going to the bottom of the key. We want presence in the tone but not hardness. A singer who does not know how to use his voice properly may create a sound that has more air than tone. We may have a similar problem on the piano, where the noise of contact with the key can diminish the pleasing quality of the tone. This is most easily heard in a soft sound or in a staccato.

The fingers are tools of the emotion as well as the intellect. Imagine how your hands would feel if you were asked to hold a fluffy, newborn chick. Now think of how your hands would feel if you were asked to hold a tiny, fuzzy spider. How would your tone at the piano differ if you were in two such different states of mind and emotion?

Consider the area of the finger that contacts the keys. I saw Alexander Siloti, Rachmaninoff's cousin, and a pupil of Liszt, come down with the whole side of his right hand to play a high note that was meant for the fifth finger and he got an incredibly beautiful tone. Josef Lhevinne believed in using the cushiony part of the finger, behind the tip, and using as large a portion of the first joint as possible, for the expressive kind of tone. The wrist needed almost always to be flexible and he referred to it as the "shock absorber."

We may use different contact areas to accommodate our expressive needs as well as the individuality of the hand. Focus on the pads of the fingertips. These cushion the fall of the fingers, acting as a spring. The pressing of them is also involved in the clinging touch and hold on the key.

You can activate this awareness by pressing each finger in turn against the thumb, or by placing the hand in playing position on a table, pressing each finger several times on the surface of the table. Feel the springiness in the cushion.

To sensitize the fingers still more, consider the sense of touch in the fingertip itself. Touch various objects very lightly and move your fingers over them. Feel their surface character. Notice the differences, for example, among smooth paper, the wood of the piano, the fabrics of different garments of clothing. Be aware of the changing sensations with each. Notice the variations in temperature among the objects. Touch the keys this way. You are awakening the sensitivity of the fingers so that you can begin to imagine them to have a sense of hearing. I often think of the violin when I play. When the violin is played, every cell in the wood vibrates and contributes to the sound. You can imagine that all the cells in your hand are open and vibrate with each sound like the wood of the violin vibrates. This imagery leads to more responsiveness in the hand and will enhance the ability to express nuances in playing. We can learn to sense ourselves as one with the instrument, picking up its vibrations as we depress the keys.

Now take a moment to examine your fingertips. Notice the pattern of ridges that make up the fingerprint. These give delicate traction to the finger; they play an important role in the clinging touch. Consideration of this helps reduce overdependence on weight, which in itself cannot give the tone expressive quality. As you play, let the weight be fed in gently, guided by the needs of your fingers so that it does not bear down and interfere with mobility.

Imagery is a fine companion to playing the piano. Sometimes I am aware of a feeling in my hand as though I were holding a paint brush, engaging only a few of its bristles, perhaps just one. When I use my fingers this way I am able to achieve a more delicate shading of volume for more tonal color.

I am sometimes so unaware of weight or conscious effort in my hands that I feel as though the keys are passing my fingers to each other. The sense of volition flows into the instrument. On occasion, in playing a tone, I may feel its sound splash up against my fingers. I may imagine a difficult but light section of music to be reflected on the surface of a body of water. I trace the movements lightly on the keys as if the image could sink.

Leschetizky said that he liked to think of the fingers as being directly attached to the shoulders. I like to extend this concept and visualize the fingers directly linked to the center of my innermost being; that place in my torso from which I draw breath, from which the emotions are expressed. The torso not only physically supports our movements at the piano; it is also the supplier of our spiritual energy. Carl Friedberg may have had something like this in mind when he stated, much more simply, "You play from your stomach."

LISTENING

I STILL REMEMBER my teacher Josef Lhevinne
saying that I needed to listen more. I was terribly frus-
trated by this remark, thinking that I was already listening
as hard as I could. Frankly, I did not know how to go about
listening any better. At that time, I did not know how to
ask the right questions which might have opened the way
to his helping me understand more deeply. I tried harder,
but what was I doing? Tensing my ear? That was all I could
think of. Even though I did not make a real inroad for
years, his words remained with me.

Some things have surfaced since that time. I remember
when I discovered silence. Silence! The mother of sound.
As a painter may portray a subject against a quiet canvas
that in its quietness still speaks to him, so it is with a
musician. What kind of silence? Is it a silence of suspense?
Or is it one of anticipation, or reflection? Is it the silence
from which is born the first sound of the composition? Is it
a silence in which the first phrase will be played once and
then be followed by another silence? The phrases may
frame the silence or the silence may frame the phrase. You

must know. When you treat a rest with indifference, you might as well have been away from the instrument during the pause getting a drink of water, for contact with the music has been lost. What follows the rest might as well be from a different piece.

Silence is as important expressively as sound. The mood felt during a silence will stand revealed. Keeping the tension of expression throughout the rest, especially in a long rest, is an art in itself. The contact from the heart of the musician to the heart of the music must not be broken, and the character of the composition exists very much in that silence. Is this rest one in which you contemplate what has just been stated? Is this rest one of reflection? Is it one in which you change character before you go on? Questioning the silences, whether they are long or short rests, or even the briefest separation between phrases, will awaken you to treat them differently.

Pausing for silence in the midst of practice allows you to mentally recreate the sounds you have just played. This internal listening can be developed. Play a segment, pause, and hear it again in your mind. Hearing the music in your head stimulates the physical impulse to play in your hands. Experienced in isolation from the act of playing, the sensations are more readily discerned. Internal listening develops both your ear and your awareness of the sensations of playing.

With the limited range of dynamics available to the clavichord and harpsichord, silence is the necessary contrast that helps create the illusion of fuller volume. The piano offers such a wide range of dynamics that players often tend to neglect the silences, and concentrate attention on tonal effects. But tonal effects cannot bring the added dimension to playing that the sensitive use of various pronunciations of silence can bring.

Many composers and performers of the 17th and 18th centuries discuss the importance of expressiveness in performance. They describe the various emotions to be evoked by the playing of long notes, short notes, and their combinations, as well as by the silences. These writers urge the instrumentalist to listen to good singers and orators in order to develop greater expressiveness in playing the instrument. The player is instructed to take a strong sense of responsibility for "reflecting every shade of feeling . . . so as to touch the heart . . . and carry the auditor from one passion to another." Some writers even suggest that each measure be of a different mood! The expression, "silences of articulation," is frequently used. Thomas Mace describes a short sound in this charming manner: " . . . as it will seem to cry 'tut' . . . so plainly as if it were a living creature, speakable."

Francesco Geminiani, an 18th century violinist, refers to a long appogiaturea and states that "it is supposed to express Love, Affection, Pleasure . . . " The violinist has the vibrato as well as the ability to increase the intensity of a long note. On the clavichord, after you have put the key down, you may increase the volume of a long note by increasing the pressure on the key. Although its volume is limited, the expressiveness of the instrument made it the favorite of Bach as well as that of many others. On the piano, the long note once played cannot be changed. Therefore, it is a greater challenge to keep the intensity of expression during the length of the note. You must be very conscious of the timing of the notes that precede and follow it, as well as the silences and the dynamic relationships to the long note.

Once you have tuned into the silences and long notes you will find all of your listening to be more keen. It will happen as a natural consequence of your own new awareness. You may find yourself listening with the skin of your fingers as well as with your whole body.

Soft practice draws in the listening focus. Within the soft sound, seek the maximum presence of tone. Strive for full expressiveness and quality even within the minimum volume. The maximum loud sound you produce should leave a margin for still more increase in volume. This will help you avoid a harsh quality, even when you are playing fortissimo chords.

When practicing chords, play each note separately and aim for full singing quality. Each finger should have a good physical sense. Think of balancing the tones when you again play them in a full chord. The vibrancy and volume will contain the essence of the singing tone and there will not be undue force.

Always try for a natural sound within any dynamic range. No matter how loud the sound the ear should not cringe. Do not mistake harshness for fullness. Josef Lhevinne often spoke of balancing every tone in a chord. In all his playing he demonstrated that no detail was too small to be worthy of investigation. When I heard him play the opening chords of the Tchaikovsky Concerto I knew how sounds of tremendous volume could have a ringing, singing resonance and still leave me feeling that he could have played them louder yet, had he wished. All the church bells in Moscow could have been ringing at once in his playing.

Think of the ideal in chamber music sound, where the balance is always delicately and sensitively proportioned. It is too easy to see a forte on the page and come down on the piano with strength, not noticing the harshness of the attack and the sharpness of the release, unless you are attuned to listening to and feeling your movement.

It is good sometimes to approach practice with the thought of listening for the best sounding tone in a phrase. Try the phrase again and see if you can spread that kind of quality throughout all the tones. Find the part that you play best in a section. See if you can tune into it in such a way as to be able to maintain that level of playing through the whole phrase. This is taking heart from your best playing. Observing your work this way makes for a more acute and involved listening and is encouraging. Stay loose and accepting so that your energy is not diverted in censorship or self-judgment. You may want to close your ears to a mistake or a phrase which displeases you, but if you know that even from a mass of failure you can extricate a few notes that were beautifully played you can use them to build your new playing. Your listening will remain open.

Listen carefully to the duration of the sounds as well as the space between the sounds. Avoid anticipating a sound. Playing a note before its time is often caused by a physical imbalance, which, in turn, is caused by lack of trust. The player may try to get into position ahead of time to be sure of covering the keys needed, and in so doing, may miss out on balancing properly along the way. The key to the difficulty may be to put the main balance not on the finger that you think, but on the one before it in preparing for a seemingly awkward change. By experiencing each sound, you will help keep yourself in balance. Anticipation can be very subtle and deceiving and you may not notice how the repose and breadth of the phrase have been upset. Each tone has a given life span. The long tones need to be given their proper due and the fast tones spaced thoughtfully, through deeply involved listening, which again, includes physical sensing.

Quantz, a famous teacher and friend of C.P.E. Bach put it this way: "However well ordered the fingers may be, they alone cannot produce musical speech." To listen profoundly seems to require a great deal of conscious effort, and at first this may be true. But gradually it will become a sensing activity in which the intellect does not monitor every move. The watchfulness is gradually absorbed in the playing. All things considered, you cannot think and then order the fingers into action. Consider a section of fast, even notes. By listening with a desire for the evenness, your fingers will be guided into an even placement, as though the ear has separated the sounds from crowding each other.

Recording your own playing, however crude and distorted the sound may be from your home recording unit, is an excellent source for self-teaching. It reflects your playing back to yourself, for in listening to the recording, the discrepancies between your wishful listening and your playing will be revealed.

SLOW PRACTICE

S LOW PRACTICE can be the most uninteresting way to spend your time at the piano—if you let it—or it can be the exact opposite. Slow practice offers the opportunity to let yourself into every crevice of the music and into the full experience of playing.

Slow practice calls for being able to sustain, in slow motion, the character of the music, which is, in itself, a high art. Slow practice allows you to carry out on a large scale the gestures used. There is time to investigate every nuance of the phrase and to realize every slight change in mood. A pattern repeated varies in expression according to its position and harmonic essence. In a long phrase of fast notes, every few notes can hint at a change of emotional nuance. Overlooking such subtleties can make the execution sound flat. In slow practice you can experience these contrasts. It is the groundwork for transforming fast note passages into fast song.

In this unhurried, unpressured kind of practice, you are more prone to separate the phrase into small segments, enabling you to pinpoint where the problems lie. Often, the cause lies in two adjoining notes. If they are not recognized, a larger portion of the work may be practiced repeatedly without overcoming the difficulty. You can be deceived as to where the problem really lies, and only by patient, loving tracing back may you see it accurately.

By practicing a small segment a few times, you may realize greater improvement than in many repetitions of the whole phrase. It is possible to jam the mind's programming by presenting it with more than one problem at a time. One inch on the page may require more difficult adjustments than twelve inches somewhere else. It is important to know how much you are really understanding. However much time your mind needs to absorb the material, that is how much time to allow yourself. Show yourself the same kind of patience that you would a good friend who could not move through the material as fast as you would wish.

In practicing slowly, I tune in entirely to where and how my hands and fingers wish to move while also exercising the most acute listening. I relax my observance of timing, allowing my fingers to linger and enjoy the changes of balance and pivoting, the subtle shifts and gestures. My fingers move with fluidity as though they had a will of their own. No movement is dictated, but is allowed to find its own way. It becomes the way of the effortless effort. I loosen the timing to free my movements and passively experience the playing. Musical intelligence is involved, but it participates permissively and passively at this stage. In a sense, it is like letting out the seams of a garment so that they will later fold back into place, fitting the wearer better than before. You are moving the playing to a level where the entire spectrum of emotions and their dynamic expressions are available.

Imagine your forearm resting and then moving on an air table. The feeling of lightness will release tremendous facility into the fingers. The more weightless the hand, the freer the movements. You will find yourself able to play fast passages with greater shading of tone. As tension is released, the arms enjoy a new ease of action. It is akin to having ball bearing action, and the difference is felt in your shoulders as well as your hands. Playing passages of fast notes can give the feeling of a gyroscope in motion.

It is very easy to lose sense of the desired balance in motion as you shift positions and cover wide areas in varied patterns of movement. Every movement has an invisible axis which is the secret of that movement. In slow practice, you can become conscious of such an axis for the hand.

Find a phrase where there is at least one shift of hand position. Play past the shift of position, playing the notes forwards and then backwards without changing the tempo. The hand naturally accommodates and adjusts, until proper tilt and balance of the hand evolve. In fast passages, the feeling is that of finding a center of centrifugal force, freeing you to enjoy the maneuvering movement. Move back and forth from a fast to slow tempo. In a slow tempo, you can also experience the balancing on each finger. When you move back into a fast tempo, be sure that no finger or tone is neglected.

Sometimes in your practice, you may suddenly find yourself trying to woo your attention back to your playing. Especially when you are working on music with which you are already acquainted, your mind may begin to wander. Often you may daydream during a piece or lose concentration without being aware of it; you may even play through an entire section before realizing it.

Becoming aware of this divided state (performing one action while the mind is elsewhere) is the first step towards improvement. As soon as you find that you are not in the center of your playing, stop. Gently release your hands and place them slowly in your lap. Interrupt the uncentered span without creating any negative feelings about it. Recognize and accept it, and you will find yourself drawn right back to your playing.

When your attention has wandered, stop on the last note or chord in a group, holding it until the sound dies away. You will feel your listening come back to the sound held. The more you are able to integrate the sensations of playing and listening, the more anemic competing thoughts will become. They will fade, leaving only the music; the listening focused back to coincide with the playing. As your attention floats back, integrating itself into the act, your body may slightly realign itself in response.

Slow practice allows your knowledge to be integrated with your playing, allowing thoughts to become feeling. It removes the interference that comes from trying to think movements into place. I like to think that all knowledge should float freely into place, finally settling as though it were a mantle of snowflakes, so light as to fit into the nooks and crannies of oneself. Slow practice is a setting in which this can take place.

FEEDBACK

I USE THE term "feedback" to mean tracing back the sensations felt in every movement made on the keys. As you become aware of the sensations felt in playing and of the muscles used, you begin to eliminate using more "horsepower" than is needed.

Place your hands in a five-finger position on the keys and without allowing the keys to move down at all, press against their surface. By applying pressure to the keys you will feel their resistance and learn how much force must be exerted in order to move them. You will also determine how much pressure you can apply against them, short of moving them. The sensory system measures the resistance of the keys as reflected in the muscle activity of the arm. In gauging the amount of force needed to move the keys, you will tune in to the tensing and relaxing of the involved muscles, and the resistance of the keys. As you press against the keys, become aware of the force you are exerting against them and the sensations felt in the hands and arms. You can feel the force

taken up in your hands and arms and trace the sensations back to your knuckles, and then to the wrist,
which gives, and to the elbows, and on up to the shoulders. The more force you exert against the keys, the
more force you will feel taken up in the hands and arms.
The shoulders shift slightly in response to the movement
against the keys. The torso gives, but is a base of support. When you cease exerting force against the keys, feel
the muscles relax. The less pressure you exert against the
keys, the lighter your touch, the more you will experience "give" throughout the arms and shoulders.

Carry this further, taking a tempo slow enough to
allow you to recognize everything that is happening as
you play. Play only on the surface of the keys, not
depressing them at all. Play so lightly that you sense the
resistance of the keys on the skin of your fingers. Allow
the feeling of resistance to be limited to your sense of
touch. Notice how your hands involuntarily adjust themselves. Now, let the whole cushion of your fingertips par-
ticipate and notice the change in feeling through your
shoulders and notice how the balance of your hands and
elbows changes. Repeat, this time allowing the keys to
depress somewhat but not enough to make a sound.
Notice how you adjust your movements to those of the
keys and how your sense of their resistance changes as
you exert more force against them.

Going through the movements used in playing in this
tranquil state makes you better able to recognize the
subtle sensations of playing. When you begin by pressing
against the surface of the keys, only gradually applying
more force, you reduce the possibility of the wrong use of
weight or pressure on the fingers which can restrict the
facility of movement. As you quiet down and are drawn
closer to your own movements, seek to discover the

points of tension, and as you focus on them your movements adjust so that the tension seems to dissolve and sensations flow more freely through the hands and arms. When the weight on the fingers is lessened, you discover a new facility and are able to move quickly and to shift through what might be awkward changes when using excess force; you sense a new confidence and trust in your own equipment. The effect is one of learning to eliminate in a passive way, the using of more horsepower than you need. I have found this to be a great help in cluing me in to the character of the action of a strange piano or even to renewing my familiarity with my own if I have not practiced for a time.

FINGERS: STRENGTH
OR ALIGNMENT

I N THE CAUSE of developing strong fingers, countless students have spent endless hours driving themselves
through exercises dedicated to developing more horsepower in their fingers than should ever be used against
the piano. A baby's hand when it grasps your finger
already has enough strength to put down the keys of a
piano. You may be able to hang from a bar by your fingers and still feel that your fingers are too weak when
you are playing. Is the problem really one of strength or
of balance and alignment?

As a child, I was able to bring my fingertips to meet
the backs of my palms and only stopped showing off this
trick when my first piano teacher frightened me by his
almost hysterical response. At the age of nine, I was
refused lessons by a very fine artist only because of this
condition. He did not believe that I could develop as a
pianist. (I did have the privilege of studying with him
after graduating from Juilliard.)

My joints remained flexible for many years, and although I did have some difficulty in finger control at

times, I refused to do the exercises that were prescribed. I ended up at a later time overcoming the whole problem in less than two weeks with only sporadic attention to it. To my own satisfaction, at least, I decided the whole business was a matter of balance and alignment.

For example, I had no problems in Ravel's *Alborada del Gracioso*, except for one B-flat. I had to play it with my fourth finger and it required a strong attack. Many times my last joint buckled and I slid off the key enough to play the lower note with it. I was very young at the time and given to anger at such occurrences. I remember sitting at the piano in a state of cold rage, deciding that the problem had to be in my head and I was going to find the source of it. I sarcastically asked myself if I could just touch the key lightly with my fourth finger without its buckling. I succeeded. Encouraged, I repeated this, all the time not pressing down on the key, just touching it. I noticed how the finger was able to hold its own position easily. Little by little, I put more weight behind the drop and the finger held the weight well. By applying my weight gradually, I developed a natural sense of alignment which I could maintain as I increased the weight. I got to the point that I could play the note fortissimo and this satisfied me. Soon after I had overcome my own problem, a twelve-year-old girl came to study with me. She showed signs of being able to learn to play very well, except for the fact that her fingers buckled at every joint. I shared my own recent experience with her and she eliminated her problem within weeks. During this period she never practiced more than half an hour a day. So it was that I became convinced that the difficulty is one of alignment and balance, and not of strength.

This conditioning can be done at odd moments as long as you have a flat surface to use. You might want to start with a book on your lap or at a table. Choose the desired shape for the finger, one that is somewhat rounded but natural. You can start with your wrist resting on the surface. At first you may, within a closed five-finger position, simply use the barest pressure and release, repeating with one finger at a time, keeping the finger in constant contact with the surface. Stop the pressure short of allowing any loss of curve at the joints; no bending in. Trace the sensation as far back as you can, in the hand, wrist, and arm. The sensation will be subtle, a barely perceptible sense of resistance. You may find it helpful to first think of the resistance at your knuckle, then back to your wrist. This can be experienced while your wrist is at rest or in motion. Next, move your thoughts to your elbow, and finally to your shoulder. This is a form of feedback. You can adjust the weight and pressure, increasing them as your finger tolerance develops.

Now at the keyboard, free the finger from its contact with the surface. Try gently tapping against the key surface, allowing your finger to move on and off the key but not allowing the key to move. Now let the key move, gently up and down, keeping your finger on the moving key. Carry this out for a repeated staccato, gradually increasing the strength of tone. Notice the changes in the sensation of resistance as you vary your movements. It is most important through the exercise to trace your sensations and to be aware of the point of control; the point at which the movement seems to originate. Allow relaxation between this point and the fingers so that the weight is adjusted to allow for freedom from unnecessary tension. This exercise can be developed for use in trill practice and any passage work. With practice, alignment will develop to the point that your sense of balance takes over where you once believed strength was required.

INNATE RHYTHM

W E ALL KNOW the teacher who sits beating on the piano with a pencil, counting aloud and directing the student to keep steady time. The student and teacher are both so concerned with keeping time that neither is listening to the tone. Tone should not have to be sacrificed to rhythm, or rhythm to tone, but all too often the pianist may end up able to keep a half-way decent rhythm having sacrificed tone sensitivity. Development of rhythm and tone can be intertwined by moving back and forth in emphasis in practice. It is possible to achieve a balance between expressiveness of sound and expressiveness of rhythm.

It is the rhythm that gives shape to the music. The most beautiful melody cannot stand on the rise and fall of pitch alone. Just as a tent falls shapeless to the ground when the stakes are removed, so would a melody fall into an unrecognizable disarray of sounds. To demonstrate this point during the course of a lesson, I have often played a familiar melody and distorted its rhythm. The student is invariably unable to recognize it.

I believe that everyone possesses innate rhythm. I have never met anyone who could not intuitively beat out a good rhythm pattern with the fingers. The difficulty of expressing rhythm on the piano is a result of all the complex functions required to transmit rhythm through the instrument. All the thinking and moving tend to interfere with the original rhythmic impulse.

It is necessary to know the divisions of measures and the subdivisions of the beat in all their formations. Numbers are used to count the beats. In the division of the beat, some teachers use their own means of designation, such as: *one-a-and-e* or *one-and-a-two-and-a* and so on. I do not believe in counting aloud while playing. The sound of numbers does not flow and does not guide the poetic rhythm of the music with ease. When we first learn the triplet rhythm, the method of counting most often used by teachers is *one-and-a, two-and-a* and so on. With a young student, I prefer instead to explain its similarity to a three-syllable phrase, such as *fiddle dee diddle dee*, saying it and having the student repeat it. We alternate in turn until the phrase comes to the student with rhythmic ease.

I suggest that the student play these syllables, saying them through the fingers on the piano. The student alternates speaking the phrase aloud with playing it until he has learned the pattern. It is much easier to feel the music through the use of *merrily merrily* or *tu-ra-la tu-ra-la* than with *one-two-three, one-and-a-two-and-a-three-and-a*. This basic idea works beautifully in all kinds of complicated rhythms that would otherwise be played with hesitation.

Quantz used to tell his students to use the sounds of the syllables *turalura (tu-ra-lu-ra)*, to feel the flow of the rhythm in a group of notes. The syllables lend a natural lilt to the grouping and accentuation that the fingers might miss in their more mechanical response to such written rhythmic combinations.

In an orchestra rehearsal, you would not be likely to hear the conductor count the phrase with numbers when he demonstrates to the players how he wants the music to sound. You would often hear a conductor use syllables like *ta-ra-ra, ta-ra-ra* or *dum-da-da, tum-da-da,* or *ti-ra ti-ra* or *dum-tum.* The conductor will choose sounds that vocally convey the rhythm that he wishes to achieve. For a particular note, he may suggest that the sound should be *tyom,* rather than *tom.* This method allows the conductor to communicate even so slight a difference. Pronouncing a sound vocally, puts you in touch with the place from which rhythm physically originates. The hand has only to follow.

It is impossible to notate timing with total precision as to the flexibility of notes within the beats. For keyboard instruments, only pitch can be notated with exactness. Indications for dynamics cannot serve as more than general suggestions, due to the many variations that can occur within a given sign. A crescendo may weaken and increase its intensity or may build directly. The dynamic indications of piano or forte may call for a greater or lesser volume of sound. The instrument and the concert hall may have their effect on your handling of the volume of tone. You will find endless considerations in realizing the flexibility possible in interpreting the markings.

The timing and the lengths of notes also cannot be indicated absolutely. Using more symbols in order to more narrowly define the rhythm would not serve the ultimate purpose since all the additional indications would only inhibit the musician's natural rhythmic expression. In natural speech, words flow in a steady rhythm that can be expressed within a beat. In between the beats, speech fluctuates subtly depending on the number of syllables and the emotional content of the words. We may linger over some words, hesitate in the midst of a phrase, suddenly rush onward at the end of a sentence. But overall we maintain a steady flow of language. Notice this in listening to the flow of natural speech.

Many compositions, while requiring the beats to fall in constant rhythm, allow for groups of notes within the beats to have the leaning and lilt of natural speech. In some works of Bach, there are pages on end full of constant sixteenth notes without letup. No one who is musically evolved would dream of playing them in that exact measurement of time. It was not meant to be so.

Another way to improve rhythmic expression is to work with just one pattern at a time. When you work with a small segment and stay with it, the effect of the improvement becomes imbedded in your memory.

As an example of what we want to emulate in rubato, consider a fine singer with a dependable accompanist. The accompanist is able to keep the rhythm moving steadily along, allowing the singer the freedom to linger or hurry as sensibilities and interpretation dictate. It would be ideal for the pianist to have the same independence in the relationship between the left and right hands. Mozart and Chopin each suggested that the left hand serve as conductor, leaving the right hand free to be rhythmically more expressive.

Practice the left hand alone and think the right hand part or sing it. Josef Lhevinne used to say that we may bend the rhythm but we must not break it. This precaution is a good one to keep in mind here. Playing the piano requires so much movement that it is sometimes easy to believe that you are playing in time when that is not quite the case. Occasionally a student may have to weather a session in which he may barely get past the second measure of a piece. This may be frustrating at the time, but will be invaluable if it teaches him how to coordinate his listening and playing. No matter what the mood to be conveyed, or how sensitive the playing, it is the rhythm that binds the expression.

THE LEFT HAND

IN MUSIC WRITTEN for the piano, the main melodic lines are almost always the highest notes the right hand plays. Even from our earliest lessons the right hand part is generally more singable than the left hand part, and we tend to carry away its tune in our minds. The left hand part is often dull, and we don't even think of it once we leave the instrument. For this reason, there is a tendency to relegate the left hand to secondary importance even as we progress, unless the left hand carries a melodic line or contains a florid passage. We may need to be reminded that no matter how insignificant a part, there is not a sound or a silence in the left hand that is not important to the whole of the music.

It was an unforgettable thrill to hear Josef Lhevinne play the *Etude in Thirds* by Chopin in a concert. It was as though he blew into this world and out again, carried on its sound. Yet, he told me that the left hand was the harder of the two. This was surprising since the left hand had single notes and moved at half the speed of the right hand which was playing in thirds. This was early in my studies with Mr. Lhevinne and I had not yet learned to respect the challenge of the simple melodic line where the playing is most exposed. I did not think of asking him to explain but I was impressed enough to be influenced in my practicing. I found myself listening for everything in the left hand that had not been obvious to me before, seeking to bring out its most subtle content as I tried to make up for past sins of neglect. It was not easy to change the habit of superficial study that had left many details unnoticed.

I would come away from a lesson thinking that nothing would escape me in this week's practice only to be shown at the following lesson that there were still more details that I had overlooked. The rewards of greater attentiveness to detail were felt not only in the left hand, inspired by Lhevinne's comment, but in all my playing.

In much of the early keyboard music of the 17th and 18th centuries used in accompanying, the written music consists of a single line of notes in the left hand. These are accompanied by numbers indicating the chords to be used with them. This style of writing is referred to as the figured bass, or continuo. Depending on the skill of the player, these chords could be strummed, or arppegiated in various ways. Bits of melody could be woven in between them and ornamented. For the very skilled player, possibilities for improvising from a figured bass were unlimited. It would be a good idea to revive this art as part of learning to play. It would serve as a medium for learning harmony and improvisation. The left hand part would become more meaningful as the student learned how it influences the music built on it.

Often a pianist plays music that could well be arranged for several musicians; there are that many melodic lines woven through it. Learning to play we develop a con-sciousness that can encompass all the parts. The sound must have full presence no matter how soft, and a rich rather than hard tone, no matter how strong.

The expression of the left hand must not be upstaged by the right hand even when it consists of lower octaves alter-nating with higher chords, as in a Chopin nocturne. In the most exquisite playing of the right hand, the total sound will be still more enhanced when the left hand supports it.

ORNAMENTS

I N THE EARLY period of keyboard history, the
use of the figured bass left the instrumentalist with a
freedom to place the chords according to taste. Only the
designated harmony and certain aesthetic rules limited
the placement. Even when the music was fully realized in
the score, some freedom was allowed for the use and
placement of ornaments, even in unindicated areas.
Cadenzas and variations upon repetition allowed for the
musician to ornament the music with diversity. A
performer had to be something of a composer, even if
only for a moment here and there. The performer's use
and composition of ornaments was an art by which he was
judged, and expression was valued more than virtuosity.

Books on performance written in the 17th and 18th centuries instruct the musician very specifically along these
lines. It was considered desirable for the ornamentation
to enhance the music with grace, not to overwhelm it. A
performer who egotistically took over a composition and
demonstrated how fast he could play the ornaments, or

how many notes he could put into a trill, was frowned upon. A musician who overloaded a piece with embellishments would be the subject of disapproval. In the 18th century, a trill interpreted simply as a show of speed was often described as the "bleating of a goat." This comparison ridiculed those performers who used ornaments to display their own facility rather than to heighten the expressiveness of the music. The eccentric use of ornamentation reached the point that composers began to put a stop to the wanton distortion of their music by indicating all the ornaments with as much precision as they could by writing out all the notes. This, in turn, created its own problem. The symbol for an ornament suggests a free filling out; an ornament fully written out becomes a fixed part of the music. The musician is more apt to play it in a calculated manner.

C.P.E. Bach recommended practicing the composition, leaving out the ornaments at first, and then fitting them in once the piece was well studied. Following his suggestion makes it easier to apply the decorative patterns in a musically intelligent manner befitting the moods of a piece. They symbols that represent the various ornaments are simply abbreviated signs for specific groups of notes. The symbol is placed above the notes to be ornamented, and indicates the kind of patterns to be used. By its size and shape the sign seems to suggest a crowding of the sounds. A symbol less than half an inch in length may suggest five or eight or more notes. If the appearance of these abbreviated signs does not mislead you into hurrying the playing, you will be more likely to play them expressively. A short ornament rapidly played in a fast moving Scarlatti sonata is fine, but the same is not necessarily true for a Bach sarabande. In other words, the same decoration should be applied differently in accord with the character of the music.

Associate the ornaments with singing, rather than fingering. Thinking of a long note, that instead of staying in one place, winds its way through several pitches, is a help in unifying the expression. A trill can be thought of in this way as well. In a slow movement, you may want to linger slightly at the start of the trill. You establish the sound and then move back and forth, increasing the speed gradually. This enables the listener to follow the sound and experience the changing continuity, without being conscious of the trill breaking into music.

Ornamentation can furnish unlimited means for varying any repetition. Some ornaments provide rhythmic vitality; some enhance the melodic line through accentuation; some add to the expressiveness of the mood conveyed by the using of several tones in the place of one. An ornament may give movement where a staying quality prevails or spread a beat to allow a sense of lingering. Passions may be expressed on the instrument with a freedom of poetic speech. Embellishment is essential to this purpose. Too often ornaments are executed with beautiful clarity and excellent division but altogether lacking the touch that would move the listener. You need only listen to a good singer in a Mozart opera to realize at once what is lacking in the emotional effects of many instrumentalists' playing. If you attempt to emulate singing, your fingers will automatically play from a different consciousness.

If you can find the opportunity to play on the clavichord or the harpsichord, you can gain more understanding and feeling for the value of ornamentation than it is possible to reach through any amount of reading or studying alone. The music of the 17th and 18th centuries takes on a different character when played on the instruments for which it was written. You will come to feel less a stranger to the music.

The sound of the attack, the duration of the sound, the release, and silences are all vitally important because of the limited range of dynamics of these instruments. The more sensitive you become to these effects, the more expressively you can fit in the ornaments. Over time and through deepening familiarity, you will develop a way of using the hand so as to draw the sweetest tone. As limited as they are in dynamic range, the harpsichord and clavichord still allow for a singing quality. The quickness of the touch plus the weight and tension of the hand are factors as are the finger movements and hand positions. Seek to allow the strings to vibrate freely.

Familiarity with these older instruments will provide a listening base from which you can learn to bring out the ornaments with more fitting expression for enriching and varying the music. Practice on them provides a framework for playing when you return to the piano.

Returning to the piano from the clavichord or harpsichord, you will not merely imitate the sound of the old instruments in a quaint manner. Instead, within the large range of dynamics of the piano, you will find a way of playing that avoids excesses of loud and soft sounds, which seeks a presence of tone that is intimate and which also has heart.

We cannot do justice to ornamentation without discussing rhythmic alteration, so important to the basic articulation of the music. You have only to look at some of Bach's music, where pages on end are full of equal sixteenth notes, to realize how important it is to have rhythmic variation. In Arnold Dolmetsch's *The Interpretation of the Music of the 17th and 18th Centuries* numerous examples are given of how the playing of a rhythmic group differed from the written music. They show various ways of playing out the different rhythmic groups. Fingering examples help facilitate the uneven playing which has the leaning and lilt of the rhythm of human speech.

As I practice ornaments, I am often reminded of a Japanese brush stroke. Just as each brush stroke is distinct and lovely in itself but integrated into the painting, the individual ornament is beautiful in itself but an integral part of the musical piece. In the same way that the Japanese painter will dedicate himself to perfecting the individual brush stroke, each of which has its own name (rat's tail, nail head, cloud longing) and character, the pianist applies the same discipline to refining the individual ornament. As I work to refine the ornaments in the context of the music, I am reminded of the discipline of the painter in his loving regard for each stroke.

IMPROVISING

F REE IMPROVISATION IS a pleasure that has been denied to too many musicians. It is often one of the first things that will be discouraged in a child. This denial is usually based on the idea that there is a prescribed and "correct" way to use the piano, and unless the child has mastered that, she has no right to use her own ideas. If a child is not intimidated at a young age, she can enjoy discovering all kinds of sound patterns on an instrument. She can develop a tremendous sense of freedom with the instrument and with her own expressiveness. It will give her a sense of friendship and intimacy with the instrument that can be acquired in no other way. It is a direct communicative experience for the child since she is directly responsible for the sounds and need not go through a waiting period for rewards.

When improvising, the child speaks to the instrument and listens to what she is saying through it. She can express what she might hesitate to say to another person. The music she makes will have none of the negative qualities to her that it might have for an older, more sophisticated, though not necessarily more sensitive ear. Unfortunately, the untimely criticism or judgment which might be brought down upon her can shatter what was a wonderful experience.

Insofar as is possible, an adult should allow the child to follow her own course. The child will create sound patterns, learn them well enough to repeat them with pleasure, and then discover new ones. At some point, the child's own ear develops, and she begins to be selective.

From this free improvisation the child may begin to compose. But that is not as important as the value of the experience itself. Whether you began to improvise as a child or only begin now as an adult, improvising will enrich all of your playing. When you learn music written by others, after having improvised yourself, you will know the process by which music comes to be and can share the feeling of creating. You will begin to enjoy playing with that most desired sensitivity: the ability to perform any work as though it were being improvised on the spot, with all the spontaneity it calls forth. Again, this can be fostered in a child if all the "teachers"—parents, other relatives, sundry adults who may not have done their own thing and now are anxious to do his—as well as the official teachers—if all these actors in his personal life will have the good grace to leave him be—to let it live. They have enough of a task in learning not to overexcite a child about his ability. They can show gentle pleasure in sharing his experience, but must not charge through the rooms of his private world like a bull in a china shop, forever to splinter his awareness, and to place the yoke of expectations on his selfhood.

Too often as a piano teacher, I have had to break through the miserable self-consciousness that has taken hold of a child before he has even had a chance. This breakthrough seems to take forever in some cases, and requires the keenest listening on the teacher's part. At the right moment, a word or phrase will begin to open up a child who has sealed off his creative self from the world. If you overlook the opportune flash of an instant, you may wait a long time for the next one.

Years ago, I approached improvisation with a seemingly repressed student. He came from a very strict home and was obedient but not spontaneous. His playing was correct but without feeling; he played as though he were a wooden soldier. I did not think that he could free himself enough to create his own individual expression. But when he began to improvise the music was unusually lovely and free. He was relaxed and enjoyed expressing himself. After my second such pleasant surprise from a prejudged student, I threw away that kind of judgment forever and realized that there is hidden beauty in everyone.

When first introducing improvisation to children, I may use a game of "Copycat." I will play a group of notes and ask the student, seated at the piano beside me, to repeat the same group. Then I may add additional notes, or increase the speed at which I play them. The child again repeats the group. In the course of the game, I will vary the patterns of notes and use different parts of the keyboard. The student builds up a certain confidence from being able to copy me and a familiarity with patterns of movement and tonal combinations. Next I let the child lead and I have to copy.

He will usually first test my tolerance for combinations of sounds by deliberately combining sounds that he expects me to find jarring. He anticipates disapproval but I accept all combinations. After all, the same jarring interval that the child discovers may be quite acceptable in a contemporary composition or may even appear in Bach in which we do not find it jarring because of the musical context. I might also ask a child to "talk" to me through the piano. I will play a phrase and have the student respond with a phrase. We might carry on a musical conversation for several minutes. Then I might ask the child to communicate with himself at the piano, allowing the right hand to speak to the left. Then I encourage him to allow both hands to speak simultaneously. I may ask him to make up a sentence and then "say" it on the piano.

If a student doesn't like the way the melody he creates sounds, I suggest that he might add a note or two in between two other notes. In this way, children are able to make up a piece before they understand notation and rhythm. In writing down their music with my help, they begin to learn notation and rhythm from their own material. Their own creations sometimes interest them more than the material in the elementary books. These same ideas can be used by an adult in experimenting with improvising.

Anyone can begin to improvise in a number of ways, and almost all who play have had a moment here and there, even if they say that they have never improvised. If you take a mistake between two notes and carry it one note further, you have already made the tiniest inroad. If, instead of going from c to d directly, you take a detour, you are already moving in the direction of improvisation. If you can't use your intuitive skill, use your imagination. If you were to make a dress and instead of sewing the collar onto the neck as indicated in the pattern, you attached it to the hem for a scalloped effect—this would be improvising.

Once you have discovered the pleasure of this free experimentation, enjoy it and don't censor or judge yourself because you will only lock up your creativity again. If you do not like what you hear, do not let yourself interfere with the process. Eventually, when you stop thinking and evaluating and can just let it happen, you will find that you have reopened an avenue for more interesting creations to come to the fore. Allow yourself this daydreaming activity. If Einstein had not been a dreamer, had he not allowed himself to feel free enough to follow his imagination unhampered, all his scientific knowledge would not have brought about his discoveries.

Out of the accidental combinations of sound that are pleasing, you have material from which to build your own musical vocabulary. You may wish to try composing a piece for your own enjoyment. Notating an idea, you can study its formation, learning to develop your spontaneous expressions into a composition.

ON READING MUSIC

O NE OF THE great pleasures of playing the piano
is sitting down with an unrehearsed piece of music
simply to make its acquaintance. Since you are not performing, there is no pressure for the playing to be flaw-
less; since you are not practicing you need not worry
about improving the weaker parts. You allow yourself to
overlook any mistakes because you do not want to interrupt the reading of the piece. At the same time, you
enjoy hearing a piece that is new to you. Part of the
musical literature opens up to you in a way different from
hearing someone else play it. You may sight read alone
or with another instrumentalist or singer. The ability to
read music fluently enhances the pleasure of playing.
Good sight reading makes it easier to learn the music
that you wish to perform and benefits your playing in
general.

Sight reading is easily developed through practice. There
are relatively few parts of musical speech, and they may
be used with such diversity as to make their juxtapositions
innumerable. With practice you learn to recognize their
formations no matter how they are arranged.

In sight reading if you find yourself conscious of working too hard, slow your pace. Seek a comfortable relationship between what the moving eye sees and the moving hand plays. If the reading remains difficult, choose simpler music. It does not matter if you must begin on a very basic level. What is important is replacing any sense of effort with a trust in *letting it happen.* The tempo should be leisurely to allow for an uninterrupted continuity of movement. If you find you need to stop, slow the speed still more. From trouble spots, pinpoint those reading problems that require your special attention. The greater number of note patterns you can recognize in quick succession, the greater your facility in playing. As you become more comfortable, you will begin to enjoy a sense of ease and be better able to hear the music as you play.

The eye combs through the printed lines of music, and the memory banks of patterns. The mind and the trained hand interact with immediacy. As your memory builds, so does the flexibility with which you respond to the patterns in music at the same instant that you see them.

The next time you're practicing sight reading, take a very quick glance at any spot on the page. Close your eyes immediately or simply look away. Play as much as you remember in that instant. As you persist in this practice, you will discover the weaknesses that prevent you from increasing your span. Once you know which note formations or patterns give you recurring difficulty, you will be able to focus on them.

If an actor were to audition for a part in a play and could not read the language fluently, how could he possibly express the character of his part? In the same way, underdeveloped reading ability stands in the way of expressing the music.

One of the joys of playing is being able to open a book and play the piano part while a friend sings or plays another instrument. This is simply making music together. It is also your rightful pleasure to make your way (however modestly) through a Chopin waltz or nocturne, a Mozart or Beethoven sonata, a work of Bach. The doors will open to endless pleasure. In this way, you acquaint yourself with all the literature you can, not needing always to think of perfecting everything you allow under your fingers.

Many accomplished pianists never develop their sight reading ability to the degree that they might and so deny themselves much pleasure. On the other hand, Rosina Lhevinne continued to play in her late eighties. When she was no longer concertizing, she spoke of how much she enjoyed having the time to read through a number of Haydn sonatas that she had never had time for earlier in her life.

TO THE ADULT
BEGINNER

THERE ARE MANY adults who, upon hearing someone play the piano, feel a stirring within themselves of an unfulfilled wish to be able to play. It is not unlike the feeling the pianist may have toward the accomplishments of others in carpentry, gardening, sewing, painting, and so on. When it comes to the piano, it is easy to believe that because of the intricate and numerous skills involved, the learning must begin in childhood. This does not take into account the fact that anything we learn to do is already partially learned before we even begin.

Some of you who have never learned to play the piano, have learned to believe that you never will, simply because you did not start as a child. If you take an inventory of some of the abilities you have developed, you may realize that it is not too late. You have developed a wealth of skills from other activities in your life. We all have this in common. We have many kinds of knowledge and many varieties of skill. The same ingredients in different relationship and proportion may be used for those new skills we would like to acquire.

When I first attempted to use a potter's wheel, I was very conscious of the importance of the sense of touch, rhythm, and even dynamics. After a few efforts, I had formed a pleasantly shaped pot. At the moment I came to the end, I was aware that the hand must be eased off gently. The slightest interference to the flowing movement will distort the shape of the pot. Regardless of the preceding efforts, that one last instant is critical. In attempting this fluid, finishing movement, I thought of how I play gradually softer in a phrase marked diminuendo. With the same feeling in my hands and in the same state of mind, I was able to successfully finish my pot.

Whenever I have tried to draw or paint, I couldn't help but be aware of the relationship to music. The involvement with composition, balance, rhythm, movement, and shading are all reminiscent of being at the piano. An adult wishing to begin playing the piano has the advantage of already knowing how to read a language. There are few letters in the musical alphabet and the organization and combination of them is very logical as is their position on the keyboard. Most adults have been exposed to music so have a store of sound combinations in the memory bank from which to draw. I believe that every movement required for playing the piano is in the repertoire of movements used in daily life. We can correlate these to the requirements of playing through gentle guidance and integration.

Your sense of hearing is already developed enough to differentiate and identify all kinds of sounds familiar to you. With a little training you can learn to differentiate and identify the individual pitches within a melody. With more practice you can carry this ability further so as to be able to distinguish the individual sounds in a chord. To

begin to develop your musical ear means to begin to develop the ability to play by ear. At first, it may be a
laborious process to find the simplest tune on the piano
but it will be rewarding to do so. Be encouraged to continue this practice. Your listening sense will be awakened
and you will find yourself more and more enjoying playing
by ear.

As an adult you have the advantage of being able to
keep a written account of your experiences at the piano.
Keep a pad and pen by the piano so that when you get a
new understanding or idea you can write it down.
Thoughts can flash by and be gone. It is worth the inter-
ruption to your practice to record these insights. You
may find that one insight will soon lead to another, and
you will enjoy delving deeper into your playing, enjoying
your self-guidance. It is very helpful to record something
of the actual sensations you experience as you play and
listen. By so doing you can help to secure and validate
newly discovered knowledge.

Recording your insights may lead you to notice a new
quality to your attentiveness. You may find yourself more
gently alert, observing from a different vantage point. It
is like being backstage, where everything that happens
may affect the activity out front. As you record your
thoughts, they may arrive with greater frequency and
fancy. The practice session becomes more and more a
time for exploring and discovery. It is a good feeling to
be able to teach yourself, seeing how far you can go with
the information provided by a teacher, taking on a greater
share of the responsibility of learning. This is one of the
benefits of learning a new skill as an adult.

Teaching an adult beginner can be as rewarding as
working with an accomplished musician. It is exciting to
observe someone discovering her own resources and

using them in new ways. I have seen what happens when an individual ceases to be in her own way and lets new skill and knowledge come together to make music.

TO HELP A CHILD

H OW DOES A young child respond to the pressures of adult expectations? What is the effect of a teacher setting the pace for the student without serious consideration of the inherent nature of this student? Often, when a child shows an interest and ability in some direction, the adults around the child take pride and begin to press for productivity. The parents look good, the teachers look good, the school looks good, and the victim, while looking good, is losing himself to others. A spiritual crime has been committed, the effects of which the child may suffer well into adulthood. The problems created by this approach may never be resolved. Although such problems exist in all fields of learning, they can be magnified in the arts. There are too many adults, who, instead of being enriched by their experience with an instrument, carry within them feelings of failure and resentment if they did not attain success and recognition in a career, or if they did not receive comforting approval from others.

Whether parent or teacher, we need to be in a constant state of learning ourselves to be able to help a child learn. This demands flexibility and self-examination. We should not decide ahead of time that a child, at any given moment, will be either receptive or resistant to what we have to offer. We may be going along blithely explaining something and be met with an expression of boredom. We need only reflect on how easily we ourselves can be bored, and how our thoughts can wander from a subject under discussion, to understand how the same thing can happen to a child. Then too, what adults identify as boredom is not always what it appears to be. It can be a façade for a child on a rapid transit trip with her own interesting thoughts. She just cannot put on the brakes and turn her attention away. Or, boredom may be the lusterless look in a child's eyes, behind which is a fear of failure, the fear of something "too hard." Boredom may hide the shame a child feels at the inability to understand. A child may mask other feelings with a façade of boredom when outside pressure and premature expectations are placed on him by parent or teacher. He may develop a fear of not meeting expectations. This can happen not only to the child who never achieves according to his parent's standards but also to the child who has done well and been overexcited by praise. It is easy to learn to need that praise.

Well-meaning adults can interfere with the beautiful and natural unfolding of a child; negative results may be felt well into adult life. Too many of our educators still insist that learning is achieved only by setting standards and using competition as an incentive. They do not see how this denies the individual pulse and tempo of the student. In fact, it may only serve to limit progress, even in the case of the student who succeeds according to a teacher's standards, not to mention the casualty who drops away in defeat. The very sensitive may even turn from success, unable to handle the heavy responsibility and pressure that comes with it. There are child labor laws, but no laws to protect the child from this sort of emotional exploitation and psychological damage. Too many adults lack the sensitivity to let knowledge flow gently; instead, they force the bud to open and violate the nature of the student.

We need to be constantly attuned to the unspoken responses of the child. He may have already learned to be dishonest for the sake of being "polite." We need to recognize that when the child says, "I do not like this piece," he may really mean, "This piece is too hard." When I guess this to be the case, I adapt the piece to the skills he already possesses. I break it down into smaller segments to allow the child to recognize patterns that are already familiar. I ease the mystery out of the unknown by analyzing its structure, and breaking it down into parts small enough that the child recognizes a relationship between it and something already learned.

A child easily overcomes difficulties when the music is appealing and familiar. Unfortunately, most children hear very little music other than what is most popular at the moment. If the disc jockeys were suddenly to push Mozart and Beethoven, what a joy that would be to the teacher! When a child is allowed to learn a piece of her choice, and her choice is often influenced by the tastes of her peers, she is quick to grasp very complex rhythms, harmonies, stretched positions, and any number of other skills in the time that she would barely master four measures of a simple, classical piece with which she is unfamiliar. Her interest draws with it her best efforts and full concentration. I think our educators would see phenomenal results if they were to drop the I.Q. tests altogether and give interest tests instead.

I remember the pure joy with which I played, improvised, and even composed music at the piano as a child. I followed my thoughts to the core of their origins and to the ends of their paths. I was the dancer, the orchestra, the music, and all in my very private world. My spirit and imagination were pliable. I could feel my whole being move in one unified direction when it was not pulled elsewhere by some adult's intrusion. I also remember the time an aunt asked me to show how well I could perform for her guests. I roughly rolled my hands up and down the keyboard. And I still recall her anger at my having let her down and my pleasure in denying her. I was four years old at the time and could play by ear. I simply enjoyed finding music on the piano.

A child is given to total absorption in his activities, even if attention is of a limited span. In light of this, I believe that a child should practice only as much as he or she wants. In this way, practice will take place as a result of the child being drawn to it. It will be done with love and involvement. Five minutes spent in this way is worth more than half an hour prescribed by teacher or parent. During an externally imposed period of practice, repetition leads to mere inattention. Conjure up a picture of the resentful victim sitting at the piano, maybe even sneakily moving the clock ahead, just as I did as a child. My thoughts were with my friends playing outdoors, or on what happened next in the adventure story from which I had been dragged. I remember sneaking the book to the piano and continuing to read, while playing away. While this may have greatly improved my sight reading ability, and my memory, I learned to operate on two tracks without giving total attention to either. It was not that I did not want to practice, but that I wanted to do it on my own terms, and only for as long as I wished. This choice was taken from me, and with it something in my nature rebelled.

The total absorption, which you can observe in any child at play, is a gift too precious to be interfered with. Once lost, it is very difficult to regain. We can help the child retain this gift by providing a healthy climate for learning, by respecting his interest, by allowing a natural pace, and by allowing him the privacy to remain intuitively centered.

TO THE STUDENT

ALL STAGES OF learning can be joyful. There is joy in new knowledge, an excitement in discovery that releases energy and enthusiasm. We welcome new ways to approach playing that can help unlock the meaning of a phrase while easing the playing of it. When we are in a continual state of learning, the same composition continues to reveal more of its hidden beauties as we continue to grow. The Lhevinnes frequently said, "When we are young we think we know everything, and as we grow older we realize that we know less and less of what there really is to know."

Many artists have re-recorded works that they recorded at an earlier age, having felt that they had so much more to say in their mature playing. It is this ever-searching quality that keeps the spirit young, even in the oldest of performers. Some of them have the opportunity to share their playing with the world even when they are in their seventies and eighties. And always there may yet remain more to be learned.

Some of you study with teachers who are renowned

within your city or throughout the world. As knowledge-able as they are, they may not always be able to articulate their knowledge. You may have to teach yourself by listening to them play, by analyzing, by watching the way they move, and by asking yourself questions. Or, they may be able to articulate their knowledge very well, but may be egotistical and insensitive to the needs of your nature. Their teaching may constitute a violation of your nature, and at some time you may have to let some knowledge drop away from you to return in a different form that is in harmony with you.

In the process of studying with such teachers, they may express themselves temperamentally and may degrade you directly or insidiously as they point out weaknesses in your playing. This is often the case with conductors and sym-phony players and can be damaging in its effect. Recognize that your teacher may be expressing his or her own under-lying weaknesses. Impatience on the teacher's part reveals an important lack in his love for the work and it is the teacher's problem. Yours is to not be victimized by it.

All knowledge has to be used with honesty. Do not put trying to please anyone else in first place, not even pleasing the teacher. You will end up trying to perform in an un-natural way, and the more you do, the more your objective will evade you. You become divided within your-self and cannot play your best.

When you hear a performance of a work that seems ideal, the temptation is to imitate. That imitation is a part of learning, a step on the way, but only that. It is a point of departure. I can remember hearing a particular recording of a work and falling in love with it. When I played the same piece afterwards, I was no longer able to play it in my own way, and yet not able to play it in the idealized man-ner to which I had been exposed. I discovered that what I liked in the recorded performance had to live in my mind until it loosened its hold and nothing remained of it but those essences which had a home within me. Reducing the whole to its essence allows for exploration and fusion. Even though some ingredients may be similar, the result has individuality and uniqueness. Instead of coming from someone else through you, it comes from you directly and is a more honest expression.

If you do not understand what the teacher is trying to impart, ask questions and keep asking until you do understand, or until you are satisfied that the teacher is incapable of explaining it.

I remember being in a harmony class and not understanding some aspect from time to time. Nobody else was asking questions, so I assumed that I was the only dummy. Finally, I got angry at myself and thought of how much was being wasted, that at a later time I would be sorry something had been left unclear. The teacher, who was brilliant, was merrily going along at a clip and was not concerning himself with the possibility that he was not being wholly understood. Perhaps in his mind he thought he would find out how much had been understood when he later gave an examination. I started to ask questions and did not allow him to go ahead until I understood. Underneath it all, I was embarrassed. When the class ended I was flabbergasted to hear that many of the other students expressed the most enthusiastic appreciation that I had asked questions, since they had understood the material even less well than I. It is too bad that the general learning environment breeds the kind of pride that stands in the way of learning. Perhaps the teacher recognized my sincere interest in the subject and was pleased to have my feedback. I know that in my own teaching, I am delighted when a student asks a question. I always interpret this as a sign that the student is interested and wants to know, and this generates more enthusiasm on my part.

Remember above all that new knowledge should always give you a feeling of enlightenment and joy. If you were to purchase a new tool which would help to do the work more easily you would hardly be able to wait to try it out. The same excitement can come with new knowledge providing there are no psycological blocks and no egotism on the part of the teacher or the pupil. If there is resistance to any new idea presented, analyze why. Otherwise, you may force the application but miss out on the benefit. You need not discard your own ideas, but you can lay them aside in reserve while trying to keep an open mind.

A new concept should be allowed to float freely through the mind without trying to grasp or capture it. It should be like seeing something with a sideward glance while the eye is in motion, instead of head on with a strained focus. As it floats free in your inner atmosphere, it will pick up something of your ways and change its contour, making its acceptance favorable to your own mental and spiritual climate.

There are many teachers whose reputation could be credited more to their students than to their teaching. If a student wins a contest, other "talents" may flock to that teacher, and soon a reputation is acquired that may be unjustified. Evaluate a teacher by what he or she can do with the "ordinary" student. This is an important point to consider. For with a class of "talented" students, the issue can become very obscure.

The delicate art of teaching should be based upon a respect for life in all its forms and an ability to relate and respond to all its beauty. Then, there need be no ordinary moment during a lesson. The teacher listens even to the unspoken word of the student, learning how best to share knowledge in a way to fit the student's individual nature.

Greed for knowledge should not interfere with the harmony of the moment. You may, in fact, have more knowledge than you can put to use. What is really needed is a spark of feeling to light its way. This may require time for quiet reflection, and self-discovery. The teacher should be willing to wait.

PERFORMANCE

K NOWING A COMPOSITION thoroughly and even mentally away from the instrument is not enough to assure that you will be free from nervousness during a performance. Too many of the world's most famous musicians have not been able to free themselves from this malady.

When I was a child, and all the way up through my teens, I performed innumerable times for large as well as small audiences, under all kinds of conditions. I would get keyed up with excitement, but I suffered no anxiety. Unfortunately, I, too, learned to be nervous. Performance anxiety developed along with my increased knowledge and my growing sense of tremendous responsibility. While I was studying at Juilliard, on fellowship with Josef Lhevinne, I became awed by the enormity of professionalism; I was suddenly aware of standards of performance that seemed far from reach. During this time, I performed seldomly so that the continuity I had established was interrupted. In trying so hard to achieve, I was forcing my development more and more. In the process of meeting these new standards, and in trying to please others, I lost my feeling of ease.

Upon graduating, I finally began to wind my way back towards my own center, making discoveries that helped me along the way. I was driven by an instinct to link the knowledge I had accumulated with my own innate feeling for playing.

Once I had experienced this joy, I began to seek it every day in practice as well as in performance. All that we are at any moment is all that we have to give. Aim for an involvement as total as can be experienced—one in which there is no room to think about the audience or critical evaluation, no room for fear of failure, or concern with success. The awareness, the engagement with the act, fills all the space.

Before beginning a performance, backstage, I go through a series of slow movements and releases very much like the ones described in this book. I find that at the same time that I am awakening the sensitivity in my arms, hands and fingers, I am quieting down.

I release each movement however slight, not forcing movement past the point where it feels blocked, where there is any hesitation. Each time I release, my breathing deepens, and my whole body seems to realign as if seeking a better posture and balance so as to support unhampered movements in the arms. Each time this body adjustment takes place, I find it easier to move more freely and over a longer span. Physically, it is as though all the senses are being tuned, and the mobility balanced. Once this body harmony is established, it seems to chase away all the tension that comes with nervousness. I am now ready to think of the music. The tension may recur but it will now be reduced. If it does recur, I go through the movements that release this tension.

Having quieted down, there is now a feeling of listening to the silence as if to locate where the music will come from; all in a very passive state. This state of being is the same as the one I need to be in to get the most beautiful tone out of the piano. This is the same condition from which the most intricate passages become attainable. What is left now is to serve the music; the music will outlive the success or failure of any single performance. When my care for the music takes over, all the other concerns have vanished along with any nervousness. In performance, we give ourselves to a command higher even than that of the critics or the audience.

While performance represents the moment of truth, it can still be one more learning experience. We learn in performance ultimate requirements which no other experience can teach us. Perhaps the most important is the purification of our attitude, freeing ourselves of external concerns that are irrelevant to making music. We learn more about the care and honesty in our work, and about being able to give ourselves to complete absorption in our playing.

O N A S N O W Y New Year's Eve in the mountains, after I had started the New Year by playing some Bach, my husband and I drove to the foot of the trail where we could look straight up at Tahquitz Peak—all granite rock. We got out of the car and simply stood still, listening to the canvas of silence through which the wind moved, playing upon the trees and anything else upon which it could spend itself. There was enough moonlight by which to see and it was in this entrancing moment that we caught the feeling of the Rock *just being*. This gave us a sense of our own just being and it was so beautiful a feeling that whenever I think back to that scene, I feel the same quietude, that same feeling of timelessness. It is this that comes to mind when I say, "Playing the piano is just one more way of being, if we let it".

BIBLIOGRAPHY

Bowie, Henry P. *On the Laws of Japanese Painting.* San Francisco: Paul Elder and Co., 1911.

Dolmetsch, Arnold. *The Interpretation of the Music of the 17th and 18th Centuries.* Edited by Ernest Newman. London: Oxford University Press, 1946.

Herrigel, Eugen. *Zen in the Art of Archery.* New York: Pantheon Books, 1953.

Lhevinne, Josef. *Basic Principles in Pianoforte Playing.* New York: Dover Publications, 1972.

Yates, Peter. *An Amateur at the Keyboard.* New York: Random House, 1964.

About the Author

M ILDRED PORTNEY CHASE began to play the piano by ear before she could speak. Her first memories of being at the piano are in her aunt's living room, picking out the melodies of songs her aunts and uncles sang. She began study at the age of five and had her own radio program at thirteen. Granted a four-year fellowship, she went on to Juilliard, where she studied with Josef Lhevinne. Later, she was featured by Peter Yates in his *Evenings on the Roof* concert series.

In recent years, the author has taught at the Los Angeles Conservatory and at the University of Southern California. Now teaching privately, she has worked with children, adult beginners, and professional musicians. JUST BEING AT THE PIANO was influenced by Eastern culture and thought. It had its inception in the journal that the author keeps by the piano to record the ever-changing process of playing the piano.